# THE SKELETON AND MOVEMENT

Brian R. Ward

Series consultant:
**Dr A. R. Maryon-Davis**
MB, BChir, MSc, MRCS, MRCP

**The Human Body**

**Franklin Watts**
London New York Sydney Toronto

© **Franklin Watts Limited 1981**

First published in Great Britain 1981
Franklin Watts Limited
12a Golden Square
London W1

First published in the United States of America by
Franklin Watts Inc.
387 Park Avenue South
New York, N.Y. 10016

UK edition: ISBN 0 85166 908 5
US edition: ISBN 0-531-04291-X
Library of Congress Catalog Card Number: 80-54826

Designed by Howard Dyke

**Acknowledgments**

The illustrations in the book were prepared by: Andrew Aloof,
Marion Appleton, Howard Dyke, David Holmes, David
Mallott, Roy Wiltshire.

# Contents

# Why we need a skeleton

Have you ever thought about why we need a **skeleton**? Just think about the meat you see in a butcher's shop. It is soft, like our own **muscle**. The other organs in our body are just as soft. Without a skeleton, we would slump into an untidy erasery heap. Our muscles are strong, but without a skeleton they have nothing to pull against and we would be unable to stand up or to move.

Some organs need more protection than others. For example, the brain and **spinal cord** are protected by the skull and the **spine**. The heart, lungs, **liver** and **intestines**

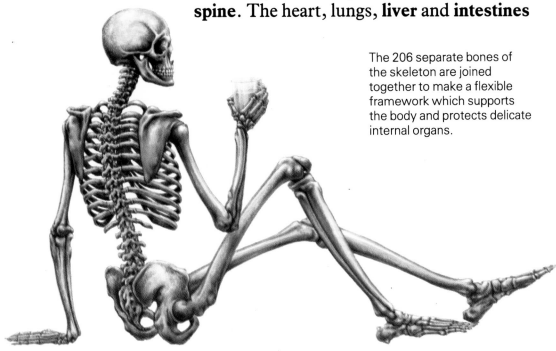

The 206 separate bones of the skeleton are joined together to make a flexible framework which supports the body and protects delicate internal organs.

4

are all easily damaged, so they are protected by ribs, hip bones and spine.

The whole system of skeleton and muscles is strong but flexible. It protects the most important organs, and allows us to move freely.

There are 206 separate bones in an adult's body. As babies we start off with about 300 bones, but some join together as we grow.

We have many more muscles than bones – about 656 separate muscles, making up a third of the total weight of a woman and nearly half the weight of a man.

With the skin removed, the hundreds of muscles which move the body can be seen. Some are very powerful; others allow delicate movement.

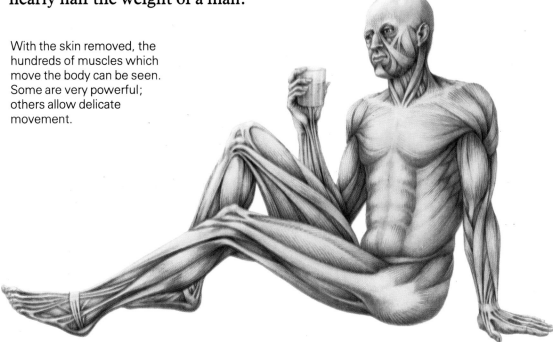

# Bones and muscles work together

The skeleton and muscles are useless without one another. They need to work together as a system if we are to be able to move as we wish. To do this they need very complicated and accurate instructions from the brain. The brain also needs information from the sense organs to tell it that the movement is being carried out properly. Close your eyes and try to touch the tip of your nose with your forefinger. You will find it difficult without using your eyes, which inform the brain exactly how the finger is moving.

The system of the skeleton and muscles is able to carry out a wide range of jobs. It may work without us realizing, such as when we automatically lean over to keep our balance as we turn a corner on a bicycle. This involves the movement of dozens of muscles, the bones of the spine, hips and shoulders, and, of course, control from the brain – all without having to think about it.

In any form of athletics the body works at its peak of performance. Tremendous strength and agility are needed, provided by the skeleton and muscles working together under the control of the nervous system.

Other physical actions do take a lot of thought, and need tremendous concentration, skill and practice. An athlete or swimmer can bring into action his or her whole skeleton and hundreds of muscles with tremendous force. A concert pianist may be using only the bones and muscles in the hands and arms, but the movements are small and delicate and timed very precisely.

# The structure of bone

The femur: the longest and strongest bone in the whole skeleton. Its upper end attaches to the hip bone; the lower end to the knee.

The framework of bones that is the human skeleton is immensely strong, yet very light.

Bones feel solid, but they are about fifty per cent water. The rest is made up of hard mineral material, mostly calcium carbonate and calcium phosphate. These are very common natural substances.

Bone develops from a white and partly transparent erasery material called **cartilage**. A baby's bones are soft and flexible, but they gradually harden as calcium passes into them. They are strengthened still more by bundles of tough stringy material called **collagen**, which runs through most of the bone. Collagen and calcium gradually disappear from the bones as we age, and in old people the bones are easily broken, because they become more brittle.

The outer part of a bone is very hard and tough, but the inside is spongy and filled with soft **marrow**. Blood vessels run into the marrow through holes in the outside of the bone, for it is here that new red blood cells are produced.

Long bones, like those in the legs and arms, are built for lightness and strength. They are immensely strong where they need to be, near the ends, while the middle part is hollow, for lightness.

All bones, except at the joints, are covered by a thin layer which contains blood vessels and special **cells** which repair damaged bone tissue.

A section through the femur shows the internal structure. Bone is a living tissue, well supplied with blood vessels.

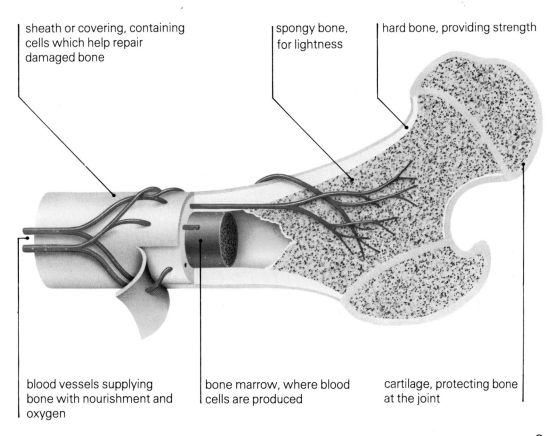

sheath or covering, containing cells which help repair damaged bone

spongy bone, for lightness

hard bone, providing strength

blood vessels supplying bone with nourishment and oxygen

bone marrow, where blood cells are produced

cartilage, protecting bone at the joint

# Cartilage, ligaments and tendons

Bones are joined together, connected to muscles, and cushioned from shock by another material – connective tissue.

One type of connective tissue is a simple packing material which fills up gaps between organs. The types important to the skeleton have one feature in common – they are all extremely tough. All connective tissue is

Structure of the knee joint. Ligaments hold the joint together, but allow free movement.

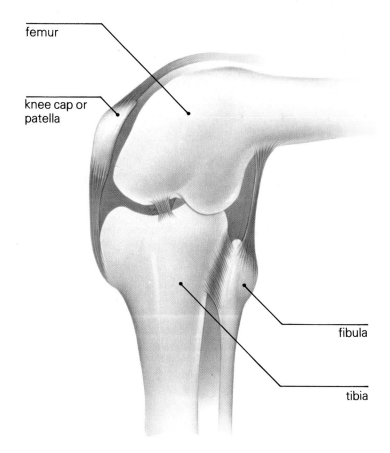

femur

knee cap or patella

fibula

tibia

made up in a similar way. It consists of a tough erasery material in which cells are embedded, together with strengthening fibers, which are either very strong white strips of collagen, or more springy yellow **elastin.**

While most of our bones gradually harden as we grow, the ends of the bones remain as cartilage all our lives and make a springy cushion at the **joints.** Cartilage is also found in other parts of the body, supporting and protecting the organs.

**Ligaments** join bones together with tough strips of tissue made up almost entirely of fibers. Ligaments hold joints together, to stop them being moved too far in the wrong direction, while allowing them to bend freely.

**Tendons** are like springy ropes, made of bundles of collagen fibers. They join muscles to bones or to other parts of the body, and enable muscles to exert a pulling action. Tendons are usually covered by a slippery sheath which helps them to move smoothly.

meniscus cartilage, frequently damaged in sports injuries

femur

ligaments

cartilage

tibia

fibula

The knee joint seen from the front. Cartilage cushions and protects the ends of the bones.

# The bones of the skull

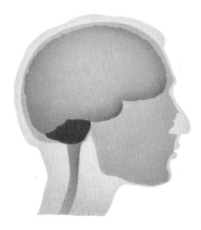

The hollow skull protects the delicate brain from damage. It completely surrounds the brain, which floats in a bath of liquid to cushion shock.

The proportions of the skull change throughout life. The rounded top part, or cranium, is large even in a child, as it has to accommodate the brain. The shape of the face and jaw changes as we grow, and in old people may still alter in shape as some bone is absorbed back into the body.

child      adult     old person

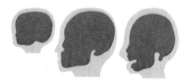

The skull is a large, roughly egg-shaped, hollow mass of bone, balanced on top of the spine.

The main part of the skull is the rounded **cranium**, which protects the brain. This is made up of eight separate bones, which in adults are joined together by rigidly fixed zig-zag joints.

In a baby these bones are still being formed and are not joined together, so that the whole cranium is slightly flexible. This allows the baby's large head to emerge safely from the mother during birth.

Gradually the bones join together as the baby grows, although there is still a soft gap at the top of the baby's head until it is about one year old.

A further fourteen bones make up the face and the jaw. Strong bones form the upper and lower jaws, into which teeth are set. The lower jaw is the only bone of the skull that moves freely. It starts life as two separate bones, which join together at the chin at about age two.

The smallest bones in the body are two sets of tiny delicate bones which are important to our sense of hearing. They are positioned deep in the ear and make up a complicated series of levers which pass sounds to the nervous system. The bones of the ear have names which refer to their shapes: hammer, anvil and stirrup.

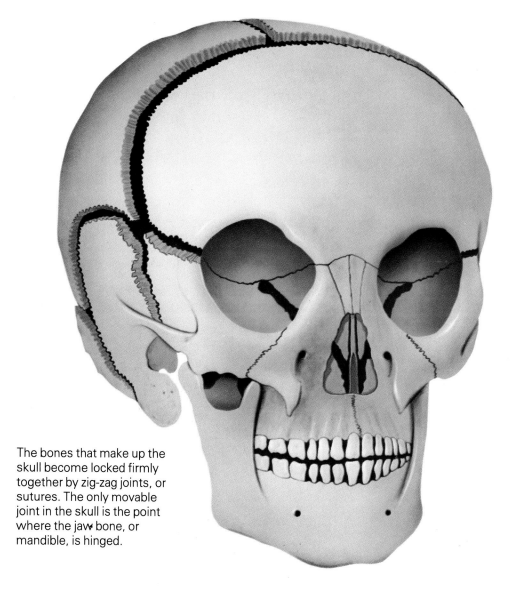

The bones that make up the skull become locked firmly together by zig-zag joints, or sutures. The only movable joint in the skull is the point where the jaw bone, or mandible, is hinged.

# The backbone

skull

atlas and axis vertebra

jaw bone

7 cervical vertebrae

12 thoracic vertebrae

disc

5 lumbar vertebrae

5 sacral vertebrae

4 vertebrae making up the coccyx

The backbone, or spine (spinal column), is a collection of thirty-three bones called **vertebrae**. They are divided into groups: the neck, upper and lower back, the hip region and a short "tail" called the **coccyx**.

The five vertebrae in the hip region are permanently fused into a single bone called the **sacrum**, while the coccyx is made up of four joined vertebrae.

Each vertebra is a complicated, ring-like shape through which the spinal cord passes. On either side is a bony spike with a longer one at the back. You can feel some of these spikes along your own back. The larger spikes, like wings, are for the attachment of ligaments and muscles.

Vertebrae are joined together by a complicated series of muscles, tendons, ligaments and cartilage. This produces a long bony tube, through which the delicate spinal cord runs, protected from harm. The spine is immensely strong, supporting the whole body. At the same time it is elastic, absorbing jolts from the legs as we walk and run. More shock protection is provided by discs of erasery cartilage between each vertebra.

The whole spine is shaped like a shallow "S," allowing it to flex easily. It is able to bend in a gentle curve, but it cannot bend sharply without damage.

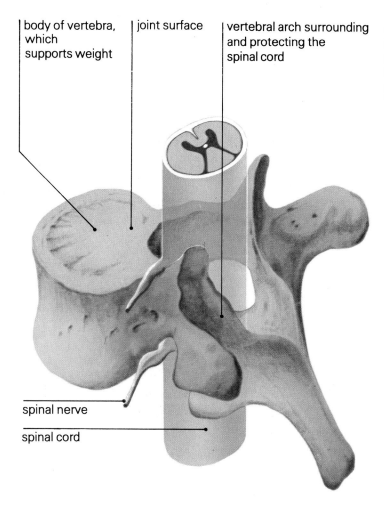

body of vertebra, which supports weight

joint surface

vertebral arch surrounding and protecting the spinal cord

A thoracic vertebra. The complicated shapes link together to form a strong but flexible spine. Muscles are attached to the protruding "wings" on the vertebra.

spinal nerve

spinal cord

# The rib cage

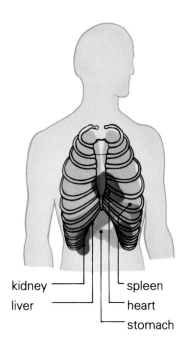

kidney — — spleen
liver — — heart
— stomach

The rib cage protects the
delicate internal organs.

The vertebrae of the upper part of the back, the thoracic vertebrae, are the attachments for the ribs. The ribs are joined to the extra-wide spines at the sides of the thoracic vertebrae.

There are twelve pairs of ribs, each attached to a vertebra at a flexible joint. The ribs are flat bones, very tough and springy, which curve toward the front of the chest, where most join on to the **sternum**, or breast bone. The bottom two short pairs are attached only to the spine – they are called floating ribs.

Beneath the sternum three pairs of ribs bend upward and are joined to each other, leaving a deep notch in the middle of the lower chest. You can feel this notch quite easily, below your ribs.

The ribs and breast bone together form the rib cage, and this has a double function. The rib cage protects the heart, lungs and the largest blood vessels in a strong basket of bone. It also helps us to breathe. Muscles run beneath the ribs, and when they shorten, or contract, they lift the whole rib cage up, increasing the size of the space inside. Air rushes into the lungs to fill this extra space. Air is then forced out again when the muscles relax and the rib cage returns to its original shape. These muscles are used in deep breathing, when the chest rises and falls noticeably. At other times, a sheet of muscle called the **diaphragm** in the **abdomen** helps to pump air in and out of the lungs.

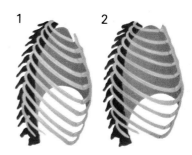

1 When lifted by intercostal muscles between the ribs, the volume of the rib cage increases and air rushes in to fill the lungs.
2 As the intercostal muscles relax, the rib cage returns to its original shape, and air is forced out of the lungs.

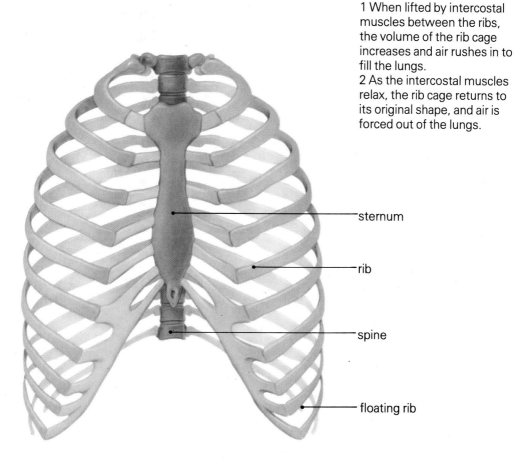

sternum

rib

spine

floating rib

# The bones of the arms and legs

The limbs, or arms and legs, of all mammals are built to a similar plan. Even the wings of bats or the flippers of dolphins look very like our own limbs when the bones and muscles are examined.

Limbs are joined to the spine by large bones, which must be strong enough to carry heavy loads and the weight of the body. In the shoulder the loads are carried by the flat **scapula**, or shoulder blade, which is held in place by powerful muscles. It is braced at the front of the shoulder by the thin **clavicle**, or collar bone, easily broken in a fall.

The limbs of all mammals are built to the same plan, although their proportions vary depending on the jobs they have to do.

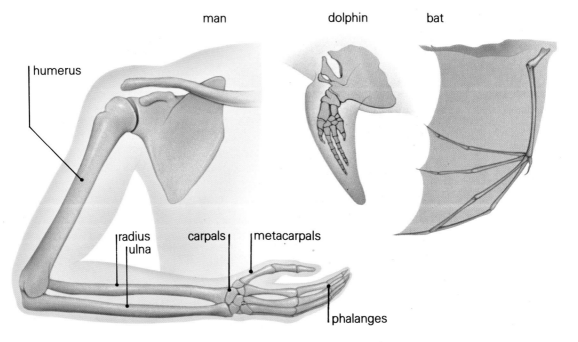

man      dolphin      bat

humerus

radius
ulna      carpals      metacarpals

phalanges

18

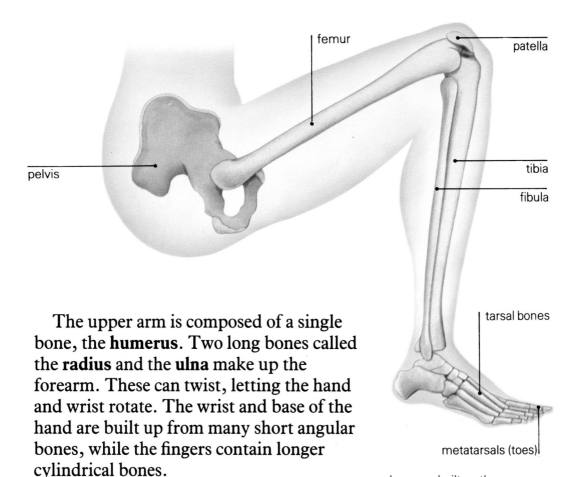

femur

patella

pelvis

tibia

fibula

tarsal bones

metatarsals (toes)

Legs are built on the same basic plan as arms, but their bones are much heavier. Legs support the whole weight of the body.

The upper arm is composed of a single bone, the **humerus**. Two long bones called the **radius** and the **ulna** make up the forearm. These can twist, letting the hand and wrist rotate. The wrist and base of the hand are built up from many short angular bones, while the fingers contain longer cylindrical bones.

Legs have a very similar structure, but the bones are more massive because they must work harder. The feet are built up like the hands, and two bones make up the foreleg – the **tibia** and **fibula**. The single **femur**, or thigh bone, has to be very strong indeed, to take our full weight when running or jumping. Its curved top is immensely strong – for its weight it is much stronger than steel – and it is the longest bone in the body. The femurs are attached to the **pelvis**. The pelvis itself consists of a pair of hip bones, which are attached firmly to the spine at the sacrum.

# Joints

Wherever two bones meet, there is a joint. Sometimes the bones are rigidly fixed together, as in most of the joints of the skull, but more frequently the joint allows the bones to move.

It is important that the bones move only in the proper direction, so the joints are built in such a way that other movements are prevented.

The joints at the knuckle allow the fingers to move only in one direction. They cannot

In the elbow a rounded spool of bone fits into a corresponding hollow, allowing movement in one direction only.

The bones of the wrist form a dome which fits into a hollow formed by the radius and ulna bones. This allows movement from side to side and back and forth.

In the spine the joint surfaces are nearly flat, allowing small amounts of sliding movement.

the hinge joint

the condyloid joint

gliding joint

humerus (upper arm)

radius and ulna (forearm)

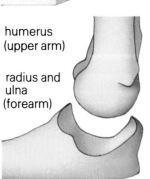

carpal bones (wrist)

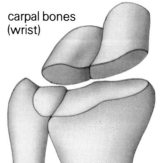

vertebrae (spine)

be twisted very far without causing some pain and damage. These joints work in the same way as an ordinary hinge.

The head moves in a different way. It can be turned from side to side, and nodded up and down. There are two special types of joint at the top of the spine – one between the skull and first vertebra, the other between the first and second vertebrae. These joints allow a wide range of movement for the head.

In the hip joint a ball on the end of the femur fits into a cup-like socket in the pelvis, allowing limited movement in all directions.

The joint at the base of the thumb allows free movement in two directions.

In this special joint at the top of the spine the ring-like atlas vertebra fits over a peg on the axis vertebra allowing the head to rotate.

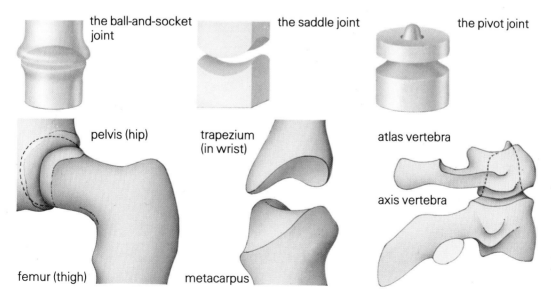

the ball-and-socket joint

the saddle joint

the pivot joint

pelvis (hip)

trapezium (in wrist)

atlas vertebra

axis vertebra

femur (thigh)

metacarpus

The joint in the shoulder is very strong, but allows the arm to move freely in any direction. The end of the long bone of the arm (the humerus) has a rounded knob which fits into a cup-shaped socket in the shoulder blade. As the ball moves in the socket, the arm can be swung freely in any direction. A very similar ball-and-socket joint connects the femur to the pelvis.

The joints between the vertebrae in the spine allow only a small amount of movement, so the spine can be rigid enough to support the body.

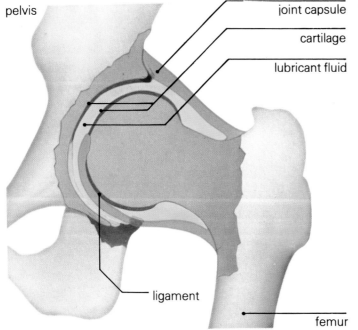

pelvis

joint capsule

cartilage

lubricant fluid

The hip joint is a ball-and-socket joint. A tough layer of cartilage covers the bones to prevent them rubbing together. Tough bands of ligaments keep the joint in place.

ligament

femur

Where bones move in a joint, some protection is needed to stop them from rubbing together.

The cartilage covering the ends of the bones is slippery and slightly erasery, like flexible plastic. This allows movement without serious rubbing. To reduce friction still more, the whole joint is surrounded by a tough bag lined with special tissue which produces a slippery liquid. This acts like oil to lubricate the joint.

Large joints in the arms and legs have to cope with shocks and jerks as we walk, run or carry out any violent movements. They need extra cushioning at the joints, and this is given by fluid-filled sacs called bursas.

The bones of the joint are held together by ligaments. These tough bands allow a certain amount of movement, while stopping the bones from moving so far that they damage the joint.

As joints move, the ends of the bones slide across each other, so it is easy to see why the surfaces of the joint must be completely smooth.

In illnesses like arthritis, the joint becomes sore and inflamed, and surfaces of the joint become roughened. This can make the joint stiff, or movement painful.

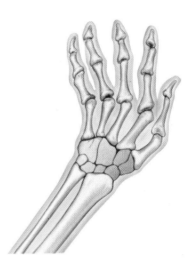

Arthritis affects the joints, particularly those in the hands. The joints become sore and inflamed and movement can be painful.

# The structure of muscles

Muscles are the key to *all* our movements. We need bones to give strength to the body, but without muscles we could not move them at all.

Muscles make up from a third to a half of our body weight, and the largest muscles are those in our legs, buttocks and arms. These are the muscles we use in our normal movement, called "skeletal" or "voluntary" muscle, but there are also other types in the body.

Smooth muscle is found in our internal organs, and in the walls of arteries. We are not usually aware of its action, as it works automatically to keep the body running steadily. One important job carried out by smooth muscle is the pushing of food along the intestine.

Cardiac or heart muscle is a very strong and tireless form of muscle. Our hearts must keep beating through our whole life, without any rest.

**Skeletal muscles** are built up from masses of tiny strands called muscle fibers, bonded together in bundles by a thin flexible skin, or **membrane**. In some muscles these fibers are up to 12 in (30 cm) long, and the muscle may consist of more than 2,000 fibers packed together. At each end of the muscle is a tough ropy tendon, which anchors the muscle firmly to bone.

Cardiac muscle is quite different. Its fibers are criss-crossed and branched, forming an untidy network rather than the neat bundles of skeletal and smooth muscle.

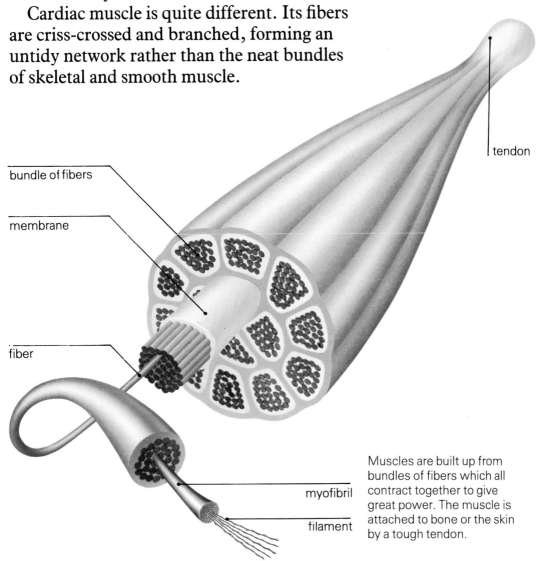

tendon

bundle of fibers

membrane

fiber

myofibril

filament

Muscles are built up from bundles of fibers which all contract together to give great power. The muscle is attached to bone or the skin by a tough tendon.

# How muscles work

Muscles have a very simple purpose. They contract, or shorten, when instructed to do so by the nervous system. A muscle contracts when the bundles of muscle fibers it contains become shorter and thicker. So the whole muscle shortens, and increases its thickness. You can see this happening when you bend your arm and tense the muscle in the upper arm.

Tiny threads branching from the nerves are buried in each muscle fiber, ending in a small flat plate. When a message is sent along the nerve telling the fiber to contract, this "motor end-plate" releases tiny amounts of a chemical which causes the muscle fiber to shorten.

The muscle fiber contains bundles of microscopic threads called **myofibrils**. They

Threads called myofibrils are responsible for contraction of the muscles. Myofibrils contain bundles of fine threads of actin and myosin, which slide toward each other to cause the muscle to contract.

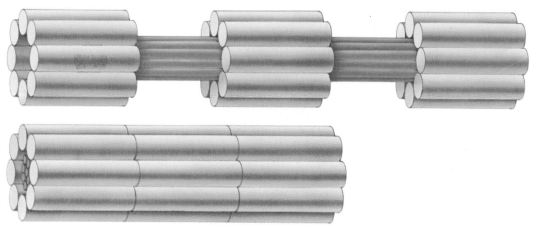

26

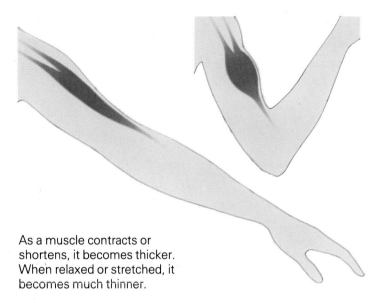

As a muscle contracts or shortens, it becomes thicker. When relaxed or stretched, it becomes much thinner.

are covered with small tooth-like structures and knobs. When the chemical messenger reaches them, two different types of myofibrils slide past each other. They grip, partly due to chemicals in the fiber, and partly because of their roughened surfaces.

The message passed to the muscle fiber is simple – it is an instruction to contract. The fiber shortens, then relaxes very quickly unless it receives another "contract" message. The more fibers that receive this message, the shorter the muscle will become, until when real muscle power is needed, almost all the fibers receive the "contract" message at the same time.

# Energy for muscles

Like a machine, muscles must be powered by energy. This energy is provided by a chemical called **ATP**, which is found all over the body. It breaks down into a simpler chemical called **ADP**, and releases energy for use by the muscles or for any other purpose. The ADP is quickly turned back into ATP, so the body always has an energy store.

In the muscle this energy powers the gripping movement of the myofibrils as the muscle fiber shortens. The use of ATP as an energy source produces several different types of waste material: water, heat, a gas called **carbon dioxide** and **lactic acid**. Carbon dioxide is removed from the body during breathing, while lactic acid is broken down by the oxygen in the air we breathe.

If we work very hard, the waste cannot be disposed of so easily. We feel hot, due to the extra heat which is produced. We pant, to flush carbon dioxide from the body. Deep breathing provides more oxygen from the air to break down the waste lactic acid. Eventually, the lactic acid may build up so much that the body cannot get rid of it quickly. The result is tiredness and aching, which clears as we rest. Then oxygen breaks down the remaining waste lactic acid.

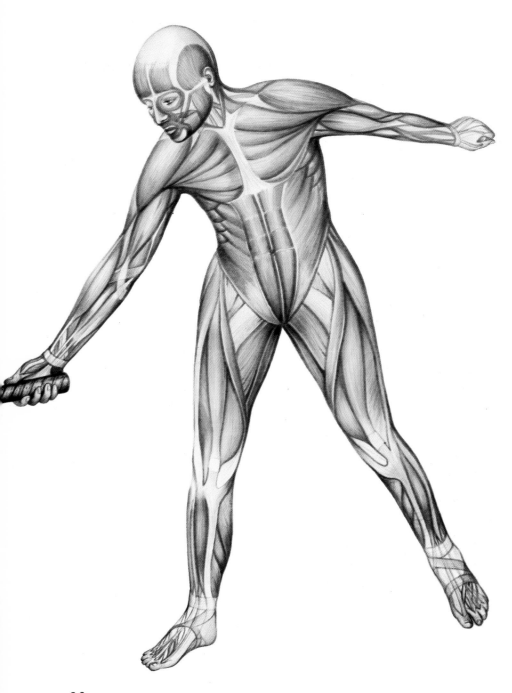

# Muscle systems

Muscles vary enormously in size. The smallest are probably the tiny muscles joining the small bones of the middle ear, inside the skull. They consist of only a few thin muscle fibers. Largest of all are the gluteus muscles, forming the buttocks.

Most muscles are paired – that is, there are identical muscles on opposite sides of the body. Skeletal muscles have several different functions, although the main ones are for movement, and to allow us to stand erect. Some are spindle-shaped, oval in section, and pointed at each end, where they connect to tendons, which are in turn anchored to bones. Other muscles are attached to the skin, where their contraction produces facial expression. Some types of muscle are attached directly to other muscles to give added power when they contract.

Muscles in the chest and upper back are used in breathing, and for moving the arms. Those running along the spine in the lower part of the back help us to stand erect. Across the stomach are thin sheets of muscle which protect the delicate organs in the abdomen.

Depending on the work they do, muscles may be flat and ribbon-shaped, fan-shaped, or in various other specialized forms.

deltoid muscle
raises the arm outward

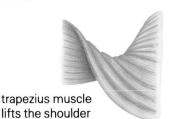

trapezius muscle
lifts the shoulder

latissimus dorsi muscle
pulls the arm down to the side

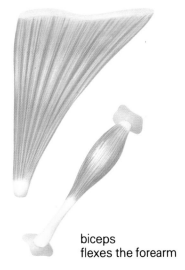

biceps
flexes the forearm

31

# Muscles as levers

Muscles move bones by the simple principle of levers. A small movement of a muscle attached near one end of a bone may cause a much bigger movement at the other end of the bone. Muscle power is transferred to the bones along tendons, some of which may be very long. Some of the muscles that move the fingers, for example, are in the forearm, and are connected to the fingers by tendons 8–10 in (20–25 cm) long.

The action of most muscles is *opposed* by another muscle. To bend or raise the forearm, the **biceps** muscle in the front of the upper arm contracts, raising the arm like a lever. To straighten the arm the **triceps** muscle, on the back of the upper arm, contracts and pulls the forearm down again.

When a muscle is completely relaxed, it is very soft, but some tension, or tone, is needed to keep the muscle healthy. A few signals from the nerves are being passed to each pair of opposing muscles all the time, keeping them both contracting gently.

Without contant use, muscles become floppy and weak, and eventually shrink in size. This often happens when a broken arm or leg is held rigid in a plaster cast while it heals. The muscle wastes away, but soon recovers its original size with exercise.

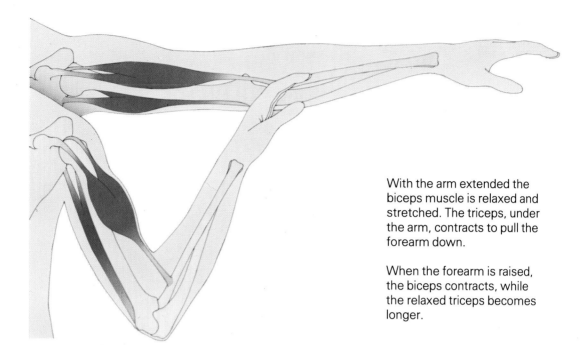

With the arm extended the biceps muscle is relaxed and stretched. The triceps, under the arm, contracts to pull the forearm down.

When the forearm is raised, the biceps contracts, while the relaxed triceps becomes longer.

The head balances on the top of the spine, on which it pivots. The weight of the head is counterbalanced by the tension of muscles at the back of the neck.

The whole weight of the body is carried on the ball of the foot, which acts as a pivot in walking. Powerful muscles at the back of the leg lift the body, using the bony heel as a lever.

The elbow joint acts as a pivot for the movement of the forearm. The weight of the forearm is raised by the biceps muscle.

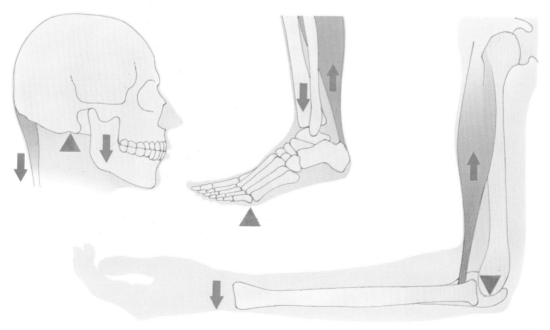

# The spinal column and the trunk

The spinal column is a complicated system of bones (vertebrae), muscles, ligaments, tendons and cartilage. All these tissues work together to produce a structure which is strong and rigid, yet at the same time capable of a certain amount of bending and twisting.

The spine, and the whole trunk, can bend backward and forward, from side to side and can rotate or twist from the hip. This movement is made possible by a large number of muscles, many of which pass along the whole length of the back.

Some muscles are attached to the hip, which acts as a secure anchor when the spine is straightened by muscular tension.

Twisting is carried out by muscles running into and around the abdomen. You can feel parts of your abdomen become tense

The structure of the spine allows bending in any direction and some twisting. The vertebrae have joints which permit this movement, while not allowing the joints to flex far enough to damage the spinal cord.

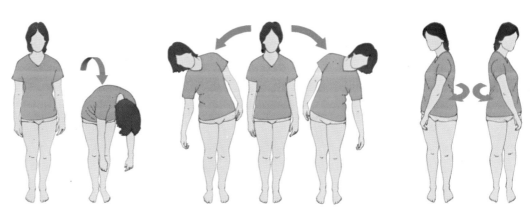

or hard as you twist your upper body.

Although the vertebrae are strapped securely together by ligaments, bending movements are still possible. This is because there is a thick disc of erasery cartilage between each pair of vertebrae. These inter-vertebral discs give slightly, to allow the spine to bend. Some of the bony projections on the vertebrae interlock and slide together as the spine bends, allowing restricted movement only in certain directions.

The spine can flex to a limited extent in any direction.

As the spine flexes, the erasery discs of cartilage between the vertebrae are compressed.

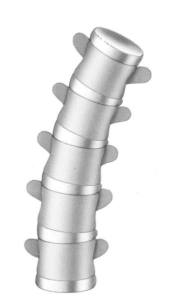

# The face and throat

Facial expressions are an important part of our everyday language. We can use expressions to signal our mood or feelings without the use of words. A smile, a frown, a wrinkled nose, or a raised eyebrow can all be used to convey a message without speaking, or they may be part of a normal conversation. We give out these signals continuously, and read them in other people,

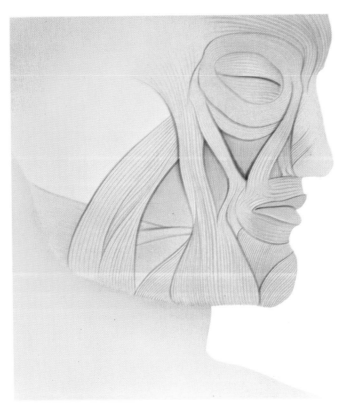

The arrangement of the muscles of the face is very complicated to provide our facial expressions and lip movements during speaking and eating. Some muscles move the whole jaw; others are attached to the skin itself.

usually without any conscious thought.

All of these examples of "body language" are controlled by the muscles of the face. There are more than thirty facial muscles, most of them attached to both the skull and the skin.

Some have very specialized purposes, such as the muscle running from the side of the face to the corner of the mouth. It pulls up the corner of the mouth to make us smile.

Another muscle runs in a flat ring around the eye, allowing the eye to be screwed up or narrowed to protect it from bright light.

Across the forehead is a whole sheet of muscle which wrinkles the forehead in a frown, and also helps raise the eyebrows.

The lips are controlled by a series of muscles to produce the accurate movements necessary for speech. The lips are the most mobile parts of the face, and can be moved in a variety of different directions.

Some muscles in the face are anchored to the skin. Their contraction moves the surface of the face, giving us a wide range of expression.

The mouth and the organs around it are capable of a very wide range of movement.

Muscles in the cheek and the side of the head move the jaw in biting, crushing and grinding actions as we eat. One set of muscles spreads out over the side of the head as far up as the temples to give extra power when clenching the teeth. Other muscles move the jaw from side to side, and back and forth.

Muscles move the jaw in three different directions: up and down for biting; to and fro and from side to side for chewing.

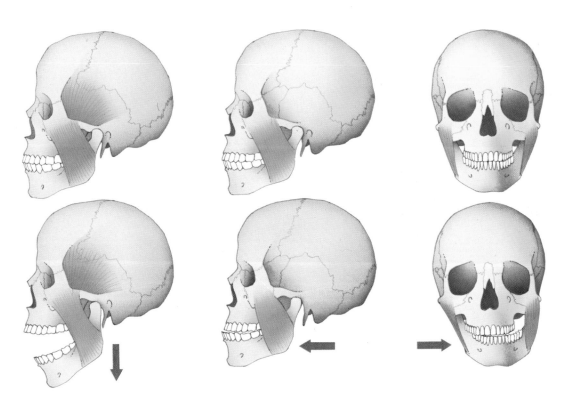

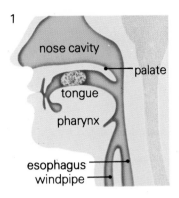

1 Food is positioned in the mouth by the muscular tongue while chewing.

The muscular lips, together with the cheeks, are also used in eating. They position food with the help of the tongue, which is itself almost all muscle. The tongue is extremely agile and capable of delicate movement. As well as its function in directing food to the teeth during chewing, it is an important organ of speech. Muscles in the roof and floor of the mouth, and in the throat, are used in swallowing.

Just below the jaw, in the upper throat, is a structure commonly called the Adam's apple, or **larynx**. This produces the sounds we use in speaking, together with the lips and tongue. The air we breathe passes through the larynx, and is used to vibrate two bands of elastic tissue – the vocal cords.

The cords are held apart during normal breathing, but when we speak, muscles pull them close together, so that the rush of air makes them vibrate to produce sounds. The muscles vary the distance between them to produce higher or deeper sounds.

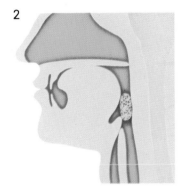

2 The tongue moves chewed food to the back of the mouth.

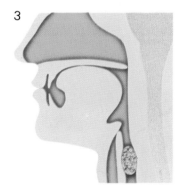

3 Once food is positioned in the gullet or esophagus, it is moved along by another set of muscles in the process called peristalsis.

# The hands and wrists

The human hand is adapted for a wide range of tasks. These may require fast movement, delicacy or powerful physical effort.

Our hands are the most useful of our organs of movement, and are finely developed tools. Machines can be built to mimic some hand movements, but it is not possible to copy their wide range of abilities.

The hands can move delicately and accurately, or fast and with considerable power. With our fingers and thumbs we can grasp objects of almost any shape and, because of our comparatively long arms, we have a very long reach.

The importance of the hands is such that a large part of the brain is used to control them. A large number of small muscles have to be controlled, and are connected to the brain by many nerves.

Several different types of joints are found in the hand and arm, to allow free but powerful movement. Simple hinge-like joints allow the fingers to move up and down, but the thumb is jointed more freely, so it can move right across the palm. This "opposed" thumb is what makes our hands so agile in picking up objects. Try to pick up a coin without using your thumb and you will see why.

In the wrist there are many small squarish bones, which allow the whole hand to swivel. The wrist can also rotate, as the two long bones in the forearm twist at the elbow joint.

To carry out all its tasks, the hand needs flexible jointed fingers and the proper muscles to move them. The hand muscles are probably the most complex and efficient in the whole body.

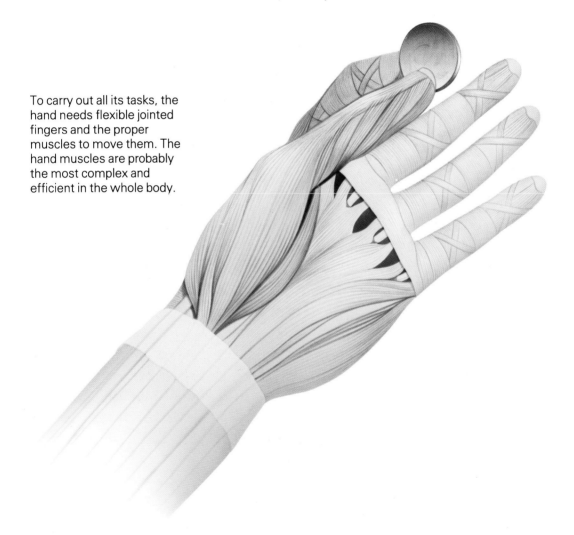

# The legs

Legs are constructed on the same basic plan as arms, but are much longer and stronger.

The length of our legs gives us extra speed when running. This in turn means that the leg bones have to be heavier and stronger to absorb the power of the muscles, and to withstand the impact of the feet on the ground.

Even a simple action such as walking actually involves a tremendous effort on the part of the nervous system, muscles and skeleton. Joints are involved all the way up the leg from the toes to the hip.

42

The muscles in the leg are extremely powerful. They not only support the weight of the body as we stand upright, but they also exert themselves even more to thrust the body forward as we run.

The bulk of the leg muscles are in the thigh, helped by those in the buttocks. These muscles do most of the work as we walk.

Muscles in the calf have a different function. They move the foot forcibly down as we stride, providing the final "push" that moves the whole body forward.

# The muscles of internal organs

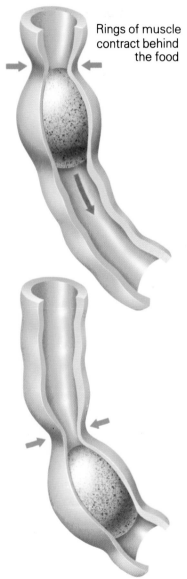

Peristalsis is the muscular process which moves food along the intestine.

Rings of muscle contract behind the food

The area of contracted muscle moves down the intestine like a wave, pushing the food material before it.

Smooth muscle, in the internal organs of the body, is sometimes also called "involuntary" muscle, because it goes on working without us consciously controlling it. This type of muscle is built up from shorter fibers than skeletal muscles. These have a slightly different structure, being pointed at each end.

Smooth muscle is usually packed in thin sheets around an organ, and contracts more gently than skeletal muscle.

Two layers of smooth muscle cover the outside of the intestine. The muscles contract to narrow the intestine behind a mass of food, then the narrowed section moves slowly along the intestine as more smooth muscle contracts. This movement, called peristalsis, forces food along the intestine like a wave.

Smooth muscle can also be seen in action in the iris of the eye. This responds almost immediately to changes in the amount of light by widening or narrowing the pupil.

The heart is mostly made up from cardiac muscle which is another form of involuntary muscle. Its rhythmic contractions are controlled by a built-in set of nerves which give a regular signal, instructing the whole mass of muscle to contract.

Skeleton and muscles work together to give us freedom of movement. The skeleton's role is simply to support the body, while allowing movement by its system of joints. The operation of muscles is immensely complicated, ranging from powerful effort, such as running, to the very delicate finger movements of the musician or surgeon. The whole body, and its movement, is overseen and controlled by the brain, and the rest of the nervous system.

# Glossary

**Abdomen:** the part of the trunk below the ribs.

**ADP:** adenosine diphosphate; a chemical present in all the tissues.

**ATP:** adenosine triphosphate; chemical which provides power to run the body. It is known as the "universal energy molecule," since it is found in all living things. It breaks down into ADP (see above), releasing energy. ADP is then recycled into ATP once more.

**Biceps:** the large muscles in the upper arm which cause the forearm to be raised.

**Carbon dioxide:** colorless gas produced as a waste product by the body, and removed through the lungs.

**Cartilage:** erasery, slippery material which lines joints, reducing friction and cushioning the bones.

**Cell:** the smallest living unit of the body.

**Clavicle:** long, thin bone running across the front of the shoulder.

**Coccyx:** tiny "tail" at the bottom of the spine. It consists of several vertebrae fused together.

**Collagen:** tough, leathery material which strengthens joints and other parts of the body.

**Cranium:** the rounded part of the skull which surrounds the brain.

**Diaphragm:** sheet of muscle and other tissue running across the abdomen just below the ribs. It is important in breathing.

**Elastin:** erasery material, present as tough threads or fibers. Found in tendons and other strong, flexible parts of the body.

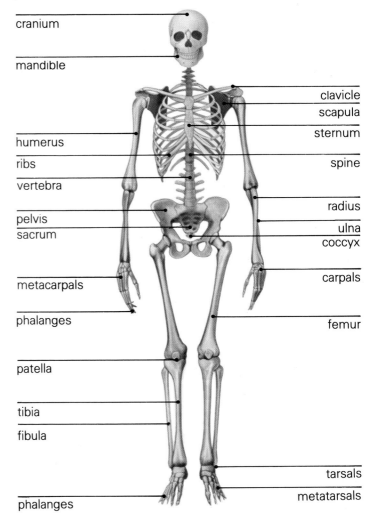

cranium

mandible

humerus

ribs

vertebra

pelvis

sacrum

metacarpals

phalanges

patella

tibia

fibula

phalanges

clavicle

scapula

sternum

spine

radius

ulna

coccyx

carpals

femur

tarsals

metatarsals

**Femur:** the thigh bone; the heaviest and strongest single bone in the body.

**Fibula:** the thinnest of the two bones in the lower part of the leg.

**Humerus:** the single bone of the upper arm. Its tip forms the elbow, or "funny bone."

**Intestines:** long muscular tube in which food is digested. The intestines include the esophagus, stomach, duodenum, small intestine, and colon.

**Joint:** the connection between bones. Some joints are firmly fixed and rigid; others allow free movement of the bones.

**Lactic acid:** chemical waste product formed in the muscles. High levels of lactic acid cause muscle tiredness.

**Larynx:** the voice box. A small box of cartilage, positioned in the neck, and containing the vocal cords. It produces sounds as air is forced from the lungs and between the vocal cords.

**Ligament:** tough ropy material which binds the bones of a joint together.

**Liver:** large organ in the upper part of the abdomen. It has several important functions, including aiding digestion, storing energy-giving materials, and making waste materials in the blood harmless.

**Marrow:** soft, fleshy tissue in the hollow center of the large bones of the body. Red blood cells are made in the bone marrow.

**Membrane:** a thin, skin-like material, which covers most of the organs of the body, both inside and out.

**Muscle:** bundle of fibers which contract together when instructed to do so by the nervous system. The muscle causes the movement of bones, or of other parts of the body.

**Myofibril:** thread-like material within muscle fibers which moves together to cause the fiber to shorten or contract.

**Pelvis:** girdle of bones made up of a pair of hip bones attached to the spine at the sacrum.

**Peristalsis:** wave-like muscular movements of the intestine which move food along during digestion.

**Radius:** one of the pair of bones in the forearm. The radius is on the same side of the arm as the thumb.

**Sacrum:** bone which connects the spine to the pelvis or hip bone. The sacrum consists of five vertebrae, permanently joined together.

**Scapula:** the shoulder blade; a large, shovel-shaped bone at the back of the shoulder.

**Skeletal muscle:** type of muscle which moves the bones of the skeleton.

**Skeleton:** the 206 bones making up the framework of the body.

**Spinal cord:** very large bundle of nerve cells running down from the brain, inside the spine.

**Spine:** the jointed backbone, consisting of thirty-three separate bones, joined together so they support the body while allowing it to bend.

**Sternum:** the breast bone; a sword-shaped bone joining the ribs at the front of the chest.

**Tendon:** tough ropy connection between a muscle and a bone.

**Thorax:** the chest; upper part of the trunk.

**Tibia:** shin bone.

**Triceps:** muscle in the upper arm which, as it contracts, extends the forearm.

**Ulna:** one of the pair of bones in the forearm, on the side opposite the thumb.

**Vertebrae:** small bones in the back, joined together to make up the spine.

# Index

48

Printed in Great Britain by Cambus Litho, East Kilbride, Scotland